Inter-Racial Love

I am the Essence of my World:
Volume One

Sang Ji

Published by Opera on Sarovar Press

First Published in Great Britain

by Opera on Sarovar Press 2018

Copyright © Sang Ji 2018

Sang Ji asserts the moral right to be identified as the author of this work.

www.sangsnotebook.com

A catalogue record for this book is available from the British Library

ISBN 978-0-9934536-4-9

Printed by CreateSpace

Published by Opera on Sarovar Press

To those whose Love
Crossed boundaries.

I know the journey
And now it is time that others know too;
Just how beautiful
This Love
Is.

Love
Is not colourblind, it is colourless;
Not faithless, but an orchestration of faith;
Not ignorant of culture, for it has enough room for everybody.

Inter-Racial Love

Other titles in this Series:

'Aap' – Water (VOL II)
Cosmology of She (VOL III)

Also by this author:

Kite Envy – I want to be Free

for Shane

CONTENTS

Sang Ji

Inter-Racial Love

1 INTER-RACIAL LOVE

We cannot talk about this love without acknowledging this fear.

It's Love that broke the mould
Not me.

I'm a slave to Love,

Willingly.

Do you even know how to spell 'love' …

Are you proud
Of your love?

I have been asked.

I felt
like a candle stood at an open window ledge:
fighting wind
(still a fire)
(still a fire).

it is disorientating.
There are levels.

And we
Are something deeper.

I cannot expect you
to realise
unless you have embedded
another world skin
within yours.

That thing
subtler than contentment, the ful of filment that combines all
and extends into flight

I am alive
and having fun

But I get a tingle
'pon my cheeks
and flutter in my belly
a warmth traces my waist
when it's him
I am coming to see.

The most natural response to love
                    Is love

Feeling love
is not the same as being it.
Animate.
Imitate.
Satiate.

Easy magic

Let it surface;
that
alarmingly beautiful
Thing

And what if two truths compete?
Can they coexist?

Love
    of all things
        was not made to be silent;

                And Courage
        cannot be grasped before it
    seeks you.

Dear Love,
Infuse our atoms, our very cells, so we can't quite think straight
or act right
          Tell …
Even
Our make up morphs into
heaven scent alleviation;
A baptism of sorts, the kind
That robs your state of mind
Frays you alive to your sensors
Housed
Underneath the vessel we call
Skin
Between the layers we
Live in
That aspect of self
Tucked within the brim
Of the cosmos.
Matter that separates;
I become
As nature intended
That which man defended
Against – deemed
So foreign
Yet felt so right
So forceful
Yet still light
Uninhibited in its might
That we almost lose
Sight
In place for
Vision that is blind in its essence
For it is the truth disguised.
Only we realise way too late
To resuscitate our (not-so) innocent lies.

Second Chances

Our love isn't any less real
Because of it.

For every time
I denied to myself that I loved you (more than
Anything)
For every time
I did not know how I should love you (more than
Anything)
I went cra-crazy inside

I could not think without
The whys
The whens and ifs
And whethers

Together forever
The prerogative
Oh how can you live
Knowing that
You knew
But didn't work it

You were

Right there, by me
So no excuses
Desired
Let lose
It

Changes
The way
You live;
look through life
At.

I would have given anything
To have my love supported
By
Love itself.

Irony does the two-step

See I know the confusion of 'should' and the interpretations of
'wisdom' by others

    how gospel is pleasily embroidered, seamlessly, sometimes.
    But the truth is not laced; you acted out of love and this is
    never ever wrong.

Ownership

Not quite touching

My feet
the ground; and I not quite reaching
my heart
I'm found

suspended
from deeper intelligence

hostage to security. Held
body contracts, melds
reacts
swells
from back here;

sometimes I dare not breathe
for fear I may give myself away
on the exhale.

do not confuse safe
with love.

Back to basics

Temper the urge to tamper the surge;
and what it means and how it holds.
We are good.

Let
Love
Be.

Wild and free and passionate. Are you *in* love if you do not
*im*press these things?

They try to tame love;
And that leaves fear out of control and free;

a Philosophy that I should be
Tamer than the two that
Made me.

Be wild and free and passionate. You are not *in* love if you do
not *im*press these things.

Texture of the L-word

But I no longer see things the way you do;
      I see things the
      Way
      Love does.

Don't they realise that falling in love
is the most precious of benevolences.
Don't they realise that staying in love

                                  and falling

over and
        falling over and
                        over and over is a pulled sacredness
  to cherisshhh ... with your life.

To love is a Calling.

yes yes yes we have hurdles
but yes yes yes yes yes yes yes yes we are more than they.

Pacing. Voicing. Unannounced. Until now

Love becomes Activist
around lovelessness.

Cause and effect

Love
Has one face

It isn't made
to Match.

Eye contact.
Levels.
Eye contact.
Depths.
Eye contact.
Searching.
Eye contact.
Found.
Eye contact.
We.

A young couple enter through the double glass doors at
Grounded Coffee, pausing – wordlessly asking – is this
the place we were looking for? The way they looked
at each other. Inter racial. Love.
She light, he dark
                    Brown.

Like

What if our fear
Suggests the same things
Our heart does; just
In Novel tongue
Twisted encryption
Its disruption undermines the
Wisdom
Generates enough friction
To blow the fuse
On our own blissdom.

So maybe think twice – or
just listen.
   Translation
   is a potent game.

Closer

The best the worst the paradox is when they do it for the sake
of you in the future;

> which is to forgo you in the now.

This isn't Love; this isn't even sense – but a complete lack of
conscious sentiment and thus loss of sacrament to the moment.

I don't know how to accept

because it is locked up tight.
The crux of the matter
For me
Is
...
And there is something going on behind the scenes.
It has wings;
And each time I try
To catch
It hovers then whizzes away;
I was half-hearted in my attempt anyway –
I could sense
The impending density of
A paper bag wound
And it is me back there,
My cells that conglomerate to commemorate
The ones we are allowed to have freely
And don't know how to
because they think it is the same as letting go,
Only
It is uncomfortable there.
And I now need
More protection from myself
Than the world outside. I can handle them.

I have come back to tell you that it's more than okay
To feel
Again.

Love,
That is doused
in the slickety thick layers of
Betrayal,
Still.
Cannot. Become it.

Love should be double-barreled and smug as hell.

p.s. I am hurt. I am scared. Vulnerable; I am human.
But my non-human knows that I am doing the right thing – the
right thing is the true thing, trumps the other right thing, known
as the good thing, the should-do-matter.

Wrestling the definition of definition

Anthropology meet metaphysics: shake hands
   with your own contortion.

Love is a way of life;
A culture of its own. An emblem of the divine.

Fear:
      whose voice are you?

Hearts don't lie;
Mirrors do.

And people, people are simply sanded statements.

Tell me your definition of 'love'

   And I can tell you
   If you know freedom.

Now, please let me own a response to the world around me.

    Appreciate that:
    My standards for love
    Are measurable astronomically;

we can love more
is what I am saying.

Love
is not
has
nothing to do with
anything else.

Do not sully it
            with ignorance
trapped in
the cursive,
captialised
and constipated.

Culture

Need I know what is wrong to say what is right?

Because. Because. Because.
Because.
Because.
Because.
Because. Because because because.

Because.

You do not
Have to prove
Your love*
To
Anyone.

Divine conscience

* can substitute 'truth' if it is so

Anointed with dew
from a tree
Made by a god
who is the same
religion as Me.

Morning walk

And I am greater for it. That makes our love greater too.

44

Truth seeks love. Or is it love that seeks the truth?
    Maybe they seek
    each other
    as perfect lovers.

Relevance

We need 'stuff'
To remind us
of what we know

Not convince us
of what we don't.

A 'true love' postcard sitting on a shelf at the coffee shop; I claimed that moment as mine.

Then I know
There is something
Worth keeping.

Cuz there
Is gold
In the vibes between us
I said
There'z gold.

> And I am the one
> Who broke it down
> When I let compare
> Tried to
> Perfect
> Something already whole.

Blink:
not the haters, but the doubters
Out.

Go with the love
That brings you peace.

Stick with the truth
That gives you faith.

The anatomy of our physiology

Maybe it is time you know about Love.

2 TRUE LOVE

You cannot delve into truth without reaching love.
(Otherwise have you delved far enough?)

I wonder what love looks like on you ...

Seeing him
Was like popping open a can of bubbly:

Sweet.

Date night

What is this thing
we have?

I love that it is labelless.

I hate it
'cos I can't fake it
when I'm with you.

There is a part of me
That is attracted to the World

Its many
Indulgences; I'd not be able to
Deduce only a few.
But
        there is a moonlit
           candy-flossed
        navel-of-a-star-ness portion
           which I share with only one.
            Only one
            Can I be
            It
            With.

A
Chemistry of Heaven.

I try everything
Ask myself: *what do you want do, eat, go, be*

When nothing works, I
Sit.
Give up trying to anything

And then it comes to me:

I simply miss him.

Boredom articulates

To find true love
Is out of my hands
Or eyes
Relies on
Parts of me
I haven't even recognised.
Until you.

Bashful

I'd be doing so well
Dancing in my shine
When your consciousness comes along
Drawing out the fullness of my journey –
Glancing where the rays dissipate;
I become this rainbow mess
That you kiss coo and caress
Until I am just me, again,
a cleansed human being.

Us: there is no escaping me, when I am with you.

which is why I find it hard
and irrefutable
to be in your arms.

And he is so soft, snug
And our passion so fierce, unyielding

that I, shaped by such forces,

am composed of
Love's spectrum.

Passionate about our love

Fizz from the bottom of the bottle rises as the lid is unscrewed.
Felt transparent as the glass it was then poured into.
Wasn't until I met his tongue did bubbles fade and waters settle.

'Love'

Because the most natural thing to do with our mouth and hands
is love.
What greater purpose are we made for?

The tenacity of our bond throws me.

I send my consciousness into space
To breathe.

Sky gazing

I wasn't sure if I needed space
        from him.
Then when I called to say good evening and good luck, I
        welled up.

Damn

You have to have softness for love.

I crack myself
Each time
I bear yolk
For you.

Us.

And it is an exquisite
expression of
Existence.

Everytime,

'til I no longer crack
But become a Balm
that runs.
Into One.

Lasting

I am found
In these extremes:
Your arms ...
The throng of
Bodies & bass.

Love listens;
    You do not even have to speak.

I need to hear
Wisdom, her pledge that
Love falls for the
Best in me.

Learned

Lessons.

>Who else
>Would I want to share them with
>>>If not you?
>Who is it worth expressing for
>If not the one who
>Lies in bed with you at
>Night.

I like having you here on Earth with me.

The words you speak
Are bubbles
On the waters of my soul.
I do not care
To understand;
I just want you.
I do not care
What you have to say;
I just want you.
Here.
Breathing against me.
Shhh.
I do not need from you
What the rest of the world
seeks –
I use words
To speed up
What I am sure you grasp from my
Gaze,
Use words to graze the atmosphere,
Pixelate
And fixate feeling
So that you know it with your human, too.
And that none of
    You
Is left out
Of our love.

Ask often and enough:

'what would love have me do?'

74

Renewing vows

He meets me
On the level
Of Real.

75

Subliminal and sublime

Let me hold you
So that I can feel
My own embrace
And know that
I still
Have it
In me.
To love.

(he calls. We share.)

And suddenly my life comes back together.

Thank You

Higher truths:
No one can rob you of the galaxy.

Innerverse

From every angle
it looks like
Love.

The coffee in my cup. 04.04.17

Bring yourself fully into focus
                    And You will find
                              My face

Miss you

Sang Ji

3 LOVE LESSONS

Pleasurable. Principled.

Love
is something
to be
done.

If there is only one thing

Stretch marks
on my heart, again:
I think it's rather
beautiful. And
necessary;
evidence of life
Itself.

The deeper the love the more voluminous your fear.
　　But there is, beneath this blessed –mess –ness,
　　An even truer expression
　　Than love.

Warm tings

Because we are not taught about love
And its force;
How it whirls vast through our bodies
Like wind, infiltrates the mind
Dominates emotions
So we fight it
Afraid
To lose control
Against our will
Yet this is its point.

If we just followed
We could reach…

It

Becomes it's-all-that-matters.

This the s**t scary state
The place
Where Love is of All – influence, consequence, significance –
        Run hide divide into your senses
        For deliverance

Love, only threatens when
We succumb to beliefs which
Imply maxims that belie
truth beyond the eye;
Or any verse that vies
We are no different from the love
Occupies
Us.

As you reach out
In an expression
Of love,
You
      spill over.

When will you realise that nothing can threaten love?
Nothing can stop it.
You cannot *do* anything to make someone not love you.

So many times
I must remind
Myself
That he is
Human.
And I can be
So
Too.

We

I crack
  Again
  And love pours through
Again.

What can be more important
than loving?

If I can love more
then I must
        – this would be my regret.

I share with him, not become him.

  Possessiveness:
a fear of separation; unaware
that distance is a reality, but not the truth.

Magic
requires
two.

Celebrate love like it's the point of life ...

Life-changing

I just
have not loved
enough.

Unsure, I tried to keep love, earn it, attain it, rather than
accepting what was already there, as mine.

Embrace

If you love in halves
How can you expect it to be
Anything less than as good as
It could be,
Spilt?

I don't know how to love
There isn't a how.

I don't know what to do.
Let love move you.

Or what to say.
Anything is made beautiful and cherishable with love.

'I am afraid to love sometimes because of how much it involves giving and not getting back.'

But experience does not denote definition.

Trap

Sang Ji

As my heart breaks

into a blue sky

And he is my prize not my purpose though he is that too;
all I can do to be better I shall so that I can keep showing you
more of me; love is purpose; I know you would love
me anyway but something about your love adorned makes
me feel bigger than I am; see it raises me up, gifts me high.

'People' cannot steal your passion –
you are the only thief in the night.

Love unfucks you up.
Prequel: love fucks you up.
Sequel: you cannot fuck love up.

Ah
The breath
Of the love
Of a caged heart.

Truly romantic;
Only.

Truth hurts. So deeply beautifully,

as the hurt becomes another confession into Love.

Remember,
too much of the mind
can blemish the heart.

They say time is money – I say time is *love*

Get richer every second giving
You expand, become
more than one
Share in blessings
Bearing fruit from anon

     Can't you feel the secret of love?

Ha! And money isn't time either – *love* is –
notice how it bides time for every second it's spent as a dime;

A Love that money can't buy & time worth saving for.

Trust is sacred.
Forgiveness, crucial.

Respect the currency.

For love to have meaning

To those in love,

because of you
I have learned
how to know.

Protect yourself with love. Allow it in abundance.

De-liberation

During
bouts of Doubt
hold
the breath

and displace it;
Not as bad as it seems
a misplaced face, it's
hardly a demon, just spectral reflection
attesting to real-time reactions
to Juxtaposed Claims
to the
Laws of the Universe.

Fact vs. Reality – versions of

Your calling
could be to
Love somebody.
Do not dismiss
This possibility
or probability.

I seek Home
whilst I am building one.

I will
show up as
Your Grace,
use all of
My faith
to be
The Love
that I
Have asked for.

Conscience of unconditional

Love Is.

If you don't believe me
You wont find out.

The order of things

4 LOVE LETTERS
Heart-stamped.

You. Wherever. Whenever.

Please keep changing
So that I can
Explore you
Over and over,

So that Sundays would never be
Just another Sunday,
But numbered,
To reflect
How many times
I have fallen for you
In this lifetime.

I don't want to ever think that I know you.

In a meeting moment
it is hard to greet you Fully;

Connect on Jupiter's tongue tip

a trip

we, a prerequisite:

Must lower myself into our vibe;
Like dipping into a bubble-filled rim

Strip and slide, a slow subside
As temperatures acclimatise.

Hello

Other days
  it's
  pausing long enough to sip a just-too-warm-to-gulp-coffee.

This is what it feels like to greet you.

Hello

And there are no words
to greet you *with*; just a need to melt into you.
This would be a true hello.

So I stay quiet and apart for a little while
till I feel
Un-phased
by the fact of our separateness.

Hello

Is there love?

Since love is not
about proving or earning,
about worthiness

the only relevant question becomes:

Is there love?

Sometimes
I cannot feel you
        Because you are so hot
        And the world is so cold
And sometimes when I get into your car
It is almost like getting frost bite. It takes time to adjust;
from meeting expectations to
just Meeting.

I miss the fights, it would hurt so much it had to be real.
I miss missing you, it hurts so much it has to be real.
I miss loving you, felt so deep mad reality feel.
I miss Our World, baby; a place a time of its own naming.
Nothing, nothing was missing. Magic, magic was dripping.
It was that complete.

Unbelievable – so it has to be real.

Loving you is baring myself,
then sharing it all with you.

My Joy

5 ACHE

Am I the only one
Who didn't receive the memo:
    Don't put love first;
    You may not have a regret
    Otherwise.

I miss him
Because I miss the part of me
He evokes
When we are together.
A part that only I, on my own, know
Intimately

Is fun to share with;
Someone I truly
Trust

Just because
My soul
Said so
Without me articulating myself.

You abandoned your soul.
They will abandon you.

This is the reflection I am living.
Except he didn't; because he knows I haven't really.

Until

I purposefully keep myself away from
    My heart
    My intelligence
    My energy
    Reality.

Until

Fuck everyone man
        - yes, yes that is pain
        right there.

The importance of defining expletives for self-development:

        'Fuck off'
        Is not rude
        But a common shield
        Against others
        And yourself
        So you do not have to explain or relate or communicate
        can just say 'fuck off'
        And it buys you some more time
        to get your shit together,
        which again means nothing
        unless you define
        'shit'.

It was only and always love. I was free when that was there.

I remember
At the beginning
I didn't try to show him that I loved him,
I just loved him.

I need to trust again that love is.
But how can it be
Unless
I am?

I feel breaches in love deeply upon my throat and psyche.

141

I was messaging my friend about where to meet for dinner she said Paddington is preferable because it would be easier for us both to get home.

Her home: the person she fell in love with.

Ache

RE: Social Sciences.

– but can they account for love? All these rhetoric and theories
what if Anomalies
could be explained
By an appreciation of human
being
compelled by capacity and conviction of heart.

Intellectualise this

The most precious commodity we have on this planet is love.
Protect it. Serve it. Service it.

144

I will listen to a whole song
Just, for that one line.
So that I can say
soundlessly, lipfully,
"yes"

This is how I know

Sometimes the pain chases desires away; glance again,
and soon pain
reveals the ones here to stay.

146

Sacrifice

If you are still together.

That love breeds
beauty in challenge overcome
every crack sealed, filled, restored.

Rough patches

After all is said and done
Yearning.

That yearning we taste last
But must satiate first
In order to
Give our lives
Order.

'*I love you*'

If
sorrow runs deep,
love runs deeper.

But tell me:
How much of our humanity
is mixed in the
Melody.
How much of our soul
Stirs with the beat.

Our Song

Can you say 'just love me' standing strong and tall and open?

These are the moments
that Faith
was made For.

Love is not a miracle;
It is natural.

6 CHOOSING

As sometimes, we must.

I recognise it.
(even from here)

That is how I know it's the truth.
That is how I know I want it too.

Yes,
I am obsessed with Love
I have chosen without realising it –
Subconscious default with reference to the soul
As purveyor of thoughts.

I am reactive to love.

Gentle warning

I am going
To find out.
Call it what you like,
There is
No greater adventure
In my opinion.

My truth
Does not depend
on your answer.

My truth
Does not depend
on your answer.

What is another word
for oxygen?

The things that give me breath

Faith requires imagination.

Loving myself is letting myself love you

164

and it feels
better.

7 WHAT NOW?

Just don't tame love. Express it. Totally and fully. Wildly and marmalade-truthfully, beautiful because it can never be harmful only deserveful and yearnful and learning comes from the expression of its lack or abundance and the balance of reciprocation is the lesson that is spun upon us now and forever more until we become all that we came for and wish to be and envy in others what is already within us ... we just don't want to be called crazy ... when the truth is, love is the antidote for its own lack. It's that easy.

Love

there is no
higher
calling.

8 ADDENDUM
Endings that trigger beginnings

it goes beyond aspiration and desire it goes beyond function and expression it is the thing that matters most in the end the thing we fight for literally but struggle against in the process because we feel we have to put something else in front of love because *if you love things will fall apart* yes they will all the shit that isn't loving taking It's rightful place will crack and blister and crumble it may well be incomprehensible your world probably will turn upside down you will go mad for a while but you will have love; it whispers to your soul somehow a calm subtle essentialism and you sync with its rhythm eventually its flow that seems senseless but is alive to you you now seem crazy to others this will test your self-esteem in the extreme because living in love is beyond the senses it isn't sense is it that this world is built on so how can love be intelligence be anything other than our enemy threatening our reality if it isn't founded on love love quite simply undermines its existence by its very own. So we have to choose. Once we stand up for love – watch can this world metamorphosise,
holding hands with the ones we do it all for.

ACKNOWLEDGEMENTS

I would like to thank to Bijou Doré for putting together the stunning book cover for Inter-Racial Love and to my graphic design technician Daniel Olabode who stitched up design glitches with no hitches. Thank you both, for being a pleasure to work with throughout.

SANG JI

is a poet and author from London, England.

www.sangsnotebook.com
@sangs_notebook (instagram)

Sang Ji